LET'S COUNT
by TANA HOBAN

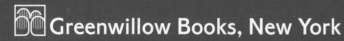 Greenwillow Books, New York

For George Ancona

The full-color photographs were reproduced from 35-mm slides.

Copyright © 1999 by Tana Hoban

All rights reserved. No part of this book may be reproduced or utilized in any form or by any means, electronic or mechanical, including photocopying, recording, or by any information storage and retrieval system, without permission in writing from the Publisher, Greenwillow Books, a division of William Morrow & Company, Inc., 1350 Avenue of the Americas, New York, NY 10019.
www.williammorrow.com

Printed in Hong Kong
by South China Printing Company (1988) Ltd.

First Edition
10 9 8 7 6 5 4 3 2 1

Library of Congress Cataloging-in-Publication Data

Hoban, Tana
Let's count / by Tana Hoban.
   p.   cm.
Summary: Photographs and dots introduce the numbers one to one hundred.
ISBN 0-688-16008-5 (trade).   ISBN 0-688-16009-3 (lib. bdg.)
1. Counting—Juvenile literature.   [1. Counting.]   I. Title.
QA113.H614 1999 513.2'11—dc21 98-44739 CIP AC

ONE

TWO

3

THREE

FOUR

5

FIVE

6

SIX

7

SEVEN

EIGHT

9

NINE

10

TEN

ELEVEN

12
TWELVE

13
THIRTEEN

FOURTEEN

FIFTEEN

20
TWENTY

30

THIRTY

40

FORTY

50

FIFTY

100

ONE HUNDRED

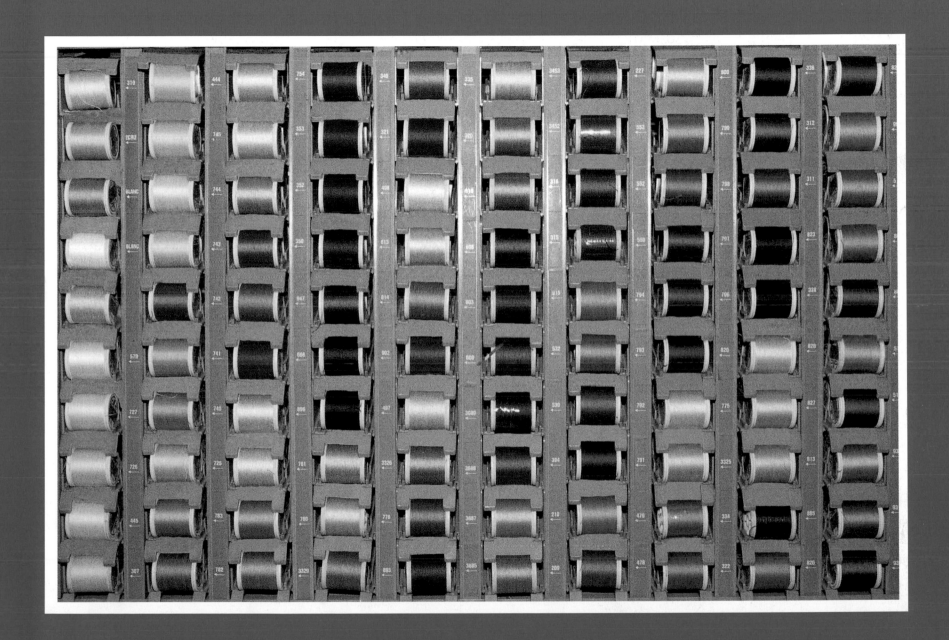